FOREWORD

Many school children will have had an English literature by being urged (or read On First Looking Into Chapman's Homer, a rightly famous sonnet by the Romantic poet John Keats. This poem (which begins "Much have I travelled in the realms of gold...") describes the light bulb moment at which the 16-year-old Keats first discovered the joys of poetry and language, the ruling passion of his tragically short life.

I must confess that, despite the great merit of being only 16 lines long, the Keats poem did not excite me the same way, but another famous publication which I chanced upon in my early teenage years most certainly did.. This title, originally published in the 18th century, before Keats was born, but remarkably still selling well 200 years later, was Hoyle's Book of Card Games, a compendium of the rules and tactics of a wide assortment of card games popular with rich and poor alike in Georgian England.

The excitement I felt on delving into an updated paperback copy of this famous title sparked a passion that has stayed with me for the rest of my life. Having started like so many children with Snap, I soon graduated to Hearts and Rummy, then on to various forms of Whist, Piquet and ultimately to Bridge, the greatest card game of them all, though one which was only invented long after the original Edward Hoyle's death.

It is difficult to exaggerate how much pleasure absorption in the joys of the card table has provided me over more than five decades. I couldn't agree more with what my polymath friend Will Sutherland says in this book about the pleasures and benefits of playing cards. The core skills you learn as a card player have proved invaluable in my own professional career. More recently, I have turned to teaching Bridge as a way of sharing and giving back to others some of what I have learned.

Of course, back in my day there were no smart phones and no computers to play games on, so cards were an easier sell than they are today. But don't be deterred. Nearly twenty years after the launch of the smartphone we are becoming more and more aware of the dangers of excessive online access and the corrosive effect of many social media platforms on young susceptible minds.

So it is definitely time for traditional card games to make a comeback. What I didn't know when I first opened up the Penguin Hoyle was that what started as a family pastime would make me so many friends and create so many happy memories in years to come. Nor did I appreciate the many enduring educational benefits; improving numeracy and reasoning, learning to harness concentration and memory, and - not least - the importance of emotional discipline. Thanks to research at the University of Stirling and elsewhere, we've also now started to appreciate that there are medical gains too, for example by inhibiting memory loss and postponing the onset of dementia.

Above all, and a point that Will makes very well in these pages, is that playing cards reminds you of the role that randomness plays in life. The younger you can learn that lesson the better and more fulfilling your life is likely to be. So please, take the clear and concise step by step guide to mastering card games and get back to play! Your children won't regret it, and nor will you.

Jonathan Davis Bridge teacher & investment professional. www.arb-oxf.uk

INTRODUCTION

On a grim winter's day 10 years ago, I was walking along the wide sweep of Embleton Bay in Northumberland and very much looking forward to a visit to the old Ship Inn. The day was cold and wet. The log burner would be warming, the beer beyond compare and the company cheerful. After removing my rain gear and picking up a pint I settled down at a table near the fire. Next to me an elderly couple were playing cards. I watched them play for 20 minutes or so as I reflected on the pleasures of good beer and a warm fire. The game they were playing – the one and only game they were playing – was **Beggar my Neighbour**. This is one of the simplest children's games because it requires no mental input of any kind!! Once the cards have been shuffled, the result is a foregone conclusion locked into the distribution of the cards. Admittedly it may take 20 minutes of play before this result becomes manifest.

You will find the rules for **Beggar my Neighbour** in a later chapter.

I got into conversation with the card-playing couple and asked them if they would like me to teach them some other simple card games. It did not take me long to explain the progression of simple card games I had found so rewarding with my own children and grandchildren. We start with **Last Card** at the age of 5 or 6 (few cards for small hands to hold and an easy way to learn suits and numbers). Next comes **Knockout Whist** (just 7 cards dealt in each hand) where they learn about *taking tricks* and the importance of *Trumps*. Once kids are comfortable with this, you can spice things up a bit with **Pelmanism** before going on to the fun and excitement of **Oh Hell**. And so the progression can continue right up to **Canasta**, **Bridge** and even **Poker**.

The elderly couple were attentive and we soon figured out how a couple of new card games worked. They thanked me for the new information and we happily parted company. I gave the incident no more thought until I happened to meet the couple again in the following year. They recognised me immediately and came over to tell me that the games I had taught them had completely transformed their relationship with their grandchildren. No more forced conversation with occasional anxious silences – the kids could not wait to play more cards with their elders. Seemingly it had never occurred to these grandparents that kids could enjoy the challenge and social contact engendered by playing games. Real games with real people really could replace addictive and vacuous addiction to screens!

It was this experience that inspired me to write this book. In my own childhood, family games had always played a big part in the way my mother's family lived. We children were the lucky beneficiaries of this as we unconsciously learned a lot about ourselves and a lot about life. Others, many others so it seemed, had not been so lucky. With the trend for modern parents to use screens as their preferred babysitters, there is now even less understanding of how games can play such a vital role in teaching children important life skills. Life is a game and not a test and it is vitally important that children understand at an early age that failure and losing are not always their fault - it's OK to lose! But if you make the best of chancy situations and use your brain to find the best solutions then you are well on the way to having a happy and successful future. The 6-year-old child that carefully studies his or her cards to choose which one to play is learning to make important and independent decisions in the micro-world of the game. These are public decisions from which there is no escape. The risks of being seen to be stupid are very real indeed, making ideal training for self-assurance in a safe space for keen young egos.

One important rule I will throw in at the start of this adventure was taught to me by a lovely Austrian au pair. ***Always end activities with kids when they are still having fun.*** If you bash on with trying to teach a new game whilst the kids are losing interest then you are going to find it that much harder to interest them in the activity next time you try.

Perhaps many modern parents will find the idea of using simple old-fashioned card games to educate their kids rather fanciful and over-blown? But there is deep wisdom as well as fun in learning to play games which in so many ways create a safe micro-version of life itself. At a time when screens and their addictive tinsel town games are dominating so many young lives, it is surely time to explore what so many previous generations have enjoyed. I hope you find the experience as rewarding as I have!

Will Sutherland
July 2024

DANCE WITH CHANCE!

All wise adults who know what's best
Know life's a game and not a test
The best laid plans of mice and men
May have results beyond our ken
The cosmic world has a sense of humour
That's really true, not just a rumour

We can't control the whims of fate
The acts of those we may love or hate
The fickle tricks of the living world
The path of history whether straight or curled
We live in nature's strange embrace
amid great inventions of the human race

So when our kids are learning stuff
The boring skills of school are not enough
To read and write is good it's true
But for lessons in life they don't give a clue
The fates can move in mysterious ways
So expecting the un-expected always pays

But how can we help our kids do well?
So in all trials of life they may excel
They need to learn that life's not fair
To dance with chance without a care
Some days you win but sometimes lose
It's no-one's fault so don't get the blues

The answer lies in their early years
If they can win or lose but shed no tears
In childhood games in small back-yards
or when you mirror life by playing cards
Exploring the power of trump and void
The lure of those screens can be destroyed

DEEP WISDOM FROM SIMPLE CARD GAMES

2. THE PLAYING FIELDS OF ETON

The Duke of Wellington was not joking when he quipped that the Battle of Waterloo was won on the playing fields of Eton. Games have always been nature's way of preparing young animals for life. By now we have all seen many TV nature documentaries which show how successful animal species learn vital life skills in the games they play when young. Whether you are a tiger, a monkey or a caribou you will learn quite automatically in playing games as youngsters the behaviours you must master to survive in the wild. Yet somehow this simple and obvious lesson seems to have been lost on most modern parents. This lesson has not been lost, of course, by the billion dollar business created by computer games. These games are carefully crafted to make them both challenging and addictive. But their dynamic and effect is very different from face-to-face games between real people. Real games between real people have an emotional and psychological content which is entirely different from the make-believe world of computer games.

A game is a safe way to explore the consequences of different types of behaviour. A game is a safe way to practise skills you will need to meet much more serious real challenges when the protection/advice of your parents/elders is no longer available. A game provides a safe way to expose yourself to the many vagaries of chance and the unexpected without catastrophic risk. A game encourages the development of social skills and inter-personal relationships (friendship!).

The famous early 20th century Russian guru Gurdjieff always pointed out the great paradox of human behaviours which tried (often successfully in the case of the rich) to eliminate all risk, discomfort and uncertainty from life. As a result, human life often became unbearably dull and without meaning. He took the view that meaning and satisfaction in life came mostly from using one's brain, experience and skill to overcome and master unforeseen challenges. This is why the man who tries to manage nature in an unpredictable garden tends to be much happier than the man who goes to the same office every day to do a job which is tediously predictable.

Seventy years ago when, as children, we were taken to have big village parties and games in the village hall we often finished with a riotous game of *musical chairs*. If 20 children got ready to play the game the adults would set out 19 chairs in a line in the middle of the dance floor. When the music started all the kids would run round and round the line of chairs waiting nervously for the music to stop. When the music stopped everyone tried to find a chair as quickly as possible because the one left standing would be eliminated from the game. As the music started again yet another chair would be removed until there was just one chair remaining for the 2 children finally left in the game. The child that jumped onto this chair when the music stopped was the winner of the game. Twenty years later when I had my own family the children were rather in two minds about this game and 20 years after that when I had my third family no children whatever would be prepared to play this game. Twenty years more went by until I was sitting next to an experienced primary school teacher during a plane flight. She explained that, at modern primary schools, sports days with races that can be won or lost are not permitted nor is she allowed to read out test results to the class in case those not doing well become too upset.

So what has been happening to change this behaviour so radically? Is it a good thing or a bad thing? That depends, of course, on your point of view. In her book **Reality is Broken** the author, Jane McGonagel, explores the reasons for the extraordinary popularity of modern video games. It seems clear that the most successful games gain their attraction precisely because they constantly pose difficult challenges which only careful thought and skill can conquer. It is the very essence of the challenge which creates the attraction of the game because modern civilised life no longer poses these sorts of challenge. Just as Gurdjieff understood more than 100 years ago that the lives of the rich had become meaningless bouts of luxury, so our modern technologies and appliances have led us to a point where challenge and danger are almost unknown. In Victorian times most families would have 5 or 6 children knowing that some would probably die in childhood. People were still acutely aware of the frailty of life, the vagaries of nature and the blessings of good luck and good judgement.

So here we are in a modern western world which has, so if seems, removed virtually all nasty risks from life. The children of modern families are born later in life and there are fewer of them so they must be protected from nasty shocks of any kind. The very idea that the natural world can (for example through storms or pandemics) bring unforeseen disaster is terrifying in the extreme. Our science and technology is supposed to have everything under control – and, if it's not already under control, then we feel sure that it soon will be. Certainly our leaders and global corporations are promoting this world view and telling us how they are going to master the next challenges whether it be climate, disease or environmental destruction.

What the Duke of Wellington had learned on the playing fields of Eton was that, in war as in life, the winners are those who cherish the challenges of the unknown and have the wit and experience to meet them. Well, you may say, you can hardly compare war to a simple card game! Here, I believe you are mistaken. In the mind of a young child, winning or losing at cards can indeed be just as BIG as winning and losing at war. Any real game, played in front of one's peers or parents, represents a micro-version of life where, whether we like it or not, there will always be winners and losers.

Here is the definition of a *game* from McGonagel's book:

A game is defined by four characteristics:
A goal or objective
A set of rules or processes
Clear and unambiguous feedback – so players know how they are doing
Voluntary participation and agreement to abide by the rules

About 3 billion people play games regularly all around the world. They spend about £250 billion each year on their games. Many of them spend almost as much time gaming as they do working.

A game gives us explicit power to do things differently.

A game tempts us to try and solve an unnecessary challenge

So, as McGonagel's book makes clear, there is no doubt that our modern existence has made video games extremely popular. The question for us now is whether simple face-to-face card games can be equally attractive and whether the face-to-face element actually adds another important and emotional dimension to this more or less safely compressed version of reality. My advice to parents and grandparents is simply to try it and see!

3. LIFE IS A GAME AND NOT A TEST

Like so many seemingly clever humans before me, I have often forgotten that life is a game and not a test. You can always pass a test (win) if you do your research and try hard enough – the same is never true of a game. Games involve chance and uncertainty with outcomes that can never be predicted however much care, practice and calculation is involved. When humans and their governments or corporations forget that all games can have uncertain and unpredictable outcomes then very dangerous mistakes can be made. In fact, most of the BIG developments in our human history have come about through what I call the mysteries of un-intended consequences. A device, behaviour, chemical or other clever invention is created to solve one problem but inevitably ends up causing some other even more disruptive and unexpected happening.

It's simply a waste of time writing any closely reasoned analysis of the many historical human disasters and mistakes – many of which came about because humans thought they had the skill and knowledge to *win* in a test against nature. The cosmos has its own way of dealing with those who cannot understand or feel the ethos of the game. We humans have a long history of opening one *Pandora's Box* after another in our misguided attempts to control the cosmos.

If, as adults, we can help our children understand from a very early age that they can use their brains and their experience to do well in games then we are giving them a wonderful gift for doing well in life. If we can show them by experience and action the difference between games and tests then we will have given them very valuable insights into the best way to approach the unforeseen challenges life will bring.

Our human story began a very long time ago – probably when we learned to use tools, control fire and make clothes. These skills gave humans a great sense of power over nature. Of course, for thousands of years the illusion of control was very limited because the great revelations of science and technology were still waiting in the wings. Humans found it necessary to believe in gods of one kind or another – the world was still a magical place. All this began to change about 200 years ago as the magic and gods were replaced by the revelations and discoveries of science and technology. Our modern civilisation began to believe that nature and the cosmos was just a huge complex machine that could be controlled by pulling the right levers. Humans began to think of themselves as "gods". Choosing the right levers and the moment to pull them was essentially a test which assumed it was theoretically possible to win by beating the *machine.* Modern humans find the idea that the cosmos may not be a *machine* - that in fact it might be dangerously wild or even have a sense of humour – VERY scary.

Modern humans are tricked by their internal picture of consciousness into believing they exist outside nature. They have the power to kill animals, mine the planet, harvest fish from the oceans and imagine that the resources of nature are there simply for their use and enjoyment. It's not popular or easy to understand that what we do to the planet we do to ourselves. Our technologies and science blind us to this obvious connection with what is ultimately an unrealistic model of the real world where orders of chance and complexity can be extreme. The reality is that at a fundamental and objective level we humans are not really *alive.* We are in fact only a very small part of our living planet and it is this planet alone that is truly *alive* as it spins in the hostile vastness of empty space.

All this philosophical musing is not something that can easily be explained in words and conversation with a young child. The only effective way to impart its important messages is by direct experience, particularly in the playing of simple games. Just for clarity, let's be clear that activities like **Chess** and **Duplicate Bridge** we sometimes hear being called games are, in fact, tests. Chance is not involved in the winning of these games because the best, most well researched and trained, minds will always win. Even in the hugely popular and well financed global sports such as football and golf, the modern players and coaches want to do everything possible to eliminate the unpredictable results of chance. Long forward passes in football are notoriously unpredictable – perhaps just a 50/50 chance the attacking side will not lose possession. This leads to the tedium of modern "possession" football. Modern golf courses are designed and maintained to reward target golf where there are no fickle bumps and bounces that might bring a very bad result from a very good shot. Modern humans tend to feel very nervous when faced with the vagaries of chance or the unpredictable behaviours of the Universe.

The planetary response to climate change is surely the final end game for this mistaken understanding of the cosmos. Twenty years after this test for humans began, we have seen governments, corporations and their tame scientists and doctors, pulling every lever they could find to control and manage the beast they believe now threatens human existence. Presidents and Prime Ministers lecture us in all the mass media with serious and determined rhetoric on the ways we will succeed in this test and "win the war against global warming". The modern human simply does not understand what every card playing child knows - *life is a game and not a test*!

The entire idea that humans can understand, control and predict the Earth's climate is a tragic symptom of misplaced confidence. One aspect of the Earth's carbon cycle nobody wants to talk about is the constant daily capture of thousands of tons of atmospheric carbon by the photosynthesis of plankton. The carbon they capture falls to the seabed as calcium carbonate (like the white cliffs of Dover) and is therefore permanently lost to the system.

This is why carbon levels in air have steadily fallen to potentially dangerous levels of less than 300 parts per million. These low carbon levels are very challenging for plant life, slowing growth and creating deserts. By putting billions of tons of carbon back into the air from burning fossil fuels humans are in fact restoring a vital element for life into the otherwise flawed carbon cycle. We can already observe that about two thirds of all this excess carbon is already being taken up by plants and plankton – greening the deserts and making our forests grow faster.

Some of us believe this confidence in the *man over nature* approach – particularly the global effort to reduce burning of fossil fuels – is very unwise. But most have simply been swept along by the ever-present fear that humans might not in fact be able to control their destiny. If life really was a "game" and not a "test", then outcomes could no longer be predicted. Games are different from tests mainly because they involve what we call "chance" - there is always a risk that careful thought and calculation may not be enough to win the game.

It should come as no surprise to learn that there is a close correlation between successful sports people and success in business. You are much more likely to succeed in life and business if you have been a successful sports person rather than just having the intellect and application to get a first-class degree. Making smart decisions quickly in the face of uncertainties and not being crushed or discouraged when they go wrong are two essential attributes for real life success. All young children are easily capable of learning this through simple card games – and, even better, have fun and get to know/respect their adult teachers at the same time!

It is very important that young children learn early that life is *not fair!* This was something I learned from my own experience with very kind and careful parents. It was always a fundamental principle of life in the Sutherland household that all goodies should be divided "fairly" between the 3 siblings (my brothers and myself). If one piece of pie or cake was left then it would be carefully divided into 3 equal pieces – sometimes on the principle of "you cut and I will choose"! This was all very fine until the day my grandfather gave us each a £10 Premium Bond. The UK Government makes a random payment/draw each month for bond holders – you could potentially become a sudden millionaire. To my parents' surprise I suddenly found myself the winner of a £100 prize. Alas, my excitement was short-lived as my careful parents informed me that my winnings must be divided up equally between the siblings. As a young teenager this determination to be "fair" struck a very harsh chord – it was my good luck to win and up to me (as I thought) to decide whether or not to share my good fortune.

When it came to bringing up my own family of 4 energetic kids, I hoped, more than anything, to bring up young people who were self-assured, confident, could think for themselves and cope well with the occasional accidents fate would throw at them. It was independence of mind that struck me as one of the most important assets. Earlier in my life I had been horrified by learning about the mind-bending techniques the German Nazi regime had used during the 1930s to whip up their own citizens into a frenzy for war. Yes, humans were certainly able to behave very like frightened sheep and the Nazi leaders were the first to realise how the power of the new mass media could be used to promote effective propaganda. The state made its own "truth" and the public meekly followed just as they did with the covid pandemic! I suppose that today we would call this dis-information – false "news" deliberately intended to deceive.

Even the simplest card games provide a scenario where independence of mind is essential – nobody is going to tell you what card to play next. When a 6-year-old child studies his/her own cards he/she is the only one facing the challenge of taking a decision about what to play! This is an important and vital first step towards independence of thought. Very soon even the youngest child barely hesitates in choosing what card to play!

Whilst independence of thought is critical to the better achievement of good outcomes in all human behaviours, we also have to learn to cope effectively with the accidents of fate. This is what I have called "dancing with chance"! If we let chance events trip us up, make us depressed or nervous of the future then we are surely destined for an unhappy life. I was determined not to make the same mistake as my parents (I probably made many other mistakes). From early days we always played games and the children learned very quickly that some days their luck might be in but other days it would be out. We reinforced this logic by tossing a coin or drawing a card to see which of the 4 kids would get the last piece of cake (or whatever). The children soon got the idea and there was no fuss or screaming apart from a few excited squeaks from the losers. Often the "winner" would share his//her prize anyway. This seemed to me to enshrine a very important lesson for life – things don't always go your way but just press on, keep calm and your luck will surely change.

4. THE BATTLE AGAINST THE SCREEN

We have all been in restaurants or airplanes where the adults are happy to hand their small children iPads or screens which essentially act "in loco parentis" or as electronic babysitters. A few years later these same parents will be struggling to manage their young child's addiction to these screens and the attractive digital alternative world they offer. In our modern world each and everyone of us must have 2 personas – a real "face to face" persona and a technologically crafted "digital" or "on line" persona. The younger you are then the greater the proportion of your emotional and social life will take place with your "on line" persona.

We don't yet know or understand what consequences this will have for the development of modern civilisation. It's still too soon to say, just as it would have been impossible to imagine the far-reaching consequences of the printing press or the motor car just 10 years after their invention. What we do know is that screens are very addictive and serve as an easy escape from the explicit challenges of "face to face" relationships. We know that Facebook "friends" are quite different from real friends We know that the clever protocols and the algorithms controlling social media produce great "echo chambers" of mis-information and hysteria. The algorithms are designed to feed you more of what you have already shown you liked. This creates highly polarised sets of opinions and political views We know "influencers" can now impact their views and opinions on many millions with just a few minutes exposure. We know that big government and big corporations now have greater power than ever to control the "narrative" as they censor the opinions and/or facts they wish to suppress.

Learning to play face-to-face games with your children is one of the best ways to compete against the attractions of the screen.

You may even find the children themselves begin to enjoy face-to-face games and the challenges and fun you can get from the more complex card games. It's easy to make sure you always have a pack of cards in your car/bag/pocket – and probably a pencil and paper too so you can keep the score.

A final word! Never be afraid to use bribery if you face resistance or apathy when the idea of cards is mentioned. The simplest form of "bribery" can simply take the form of saying "well done" or "brilliant". All intelligent creatures respond to rewards rather than threats. This was a lesson I learned from a colleague who had just come back from a stay with her sister who was a dolphin trainer in Florida. Dolphins are clever and they crave excitement and attention. Very often they will "mis-behave" if things are not going well. If you try to punish them this is simply another way they can get the stimulation they are wanting – they will mis-behave even more! But if you are able to completely ignore the bad behaviours and give encouragement and rewards for even the smallest efforts at "good" behaviours then you will slowly but steadily achieve the results you want. Exactly the same is true of your children or even your husband/wife!

5. WHERE TO START?

It is certainly not possible to say at what age a child will find card games possible or interesting but it is possible to say that they will not be able to hold a full hand of 13 cards (or more in the case of **Canasta**) with a very small hand. This is one advantage of starting with games like **Last Card** or **Knockout Whist** where the initial hand is 5 or 7 cards respectively. We need to make sure small people are happy to hold up their hands comfortably so they don't battle to organise them and don't find it difficult to keep their cards hidden from other players. You can make a card-holding device by covering a couple of old CDs with cloth and sticking them together so cards can be stuck into the edges!

It's always a good idea to play cards with sensible chairs and a table which is either covered with card-playing baize or has a cloth put over it so cards can be picked up easily without scrabbling about with finger nails. Cards need to be shuffled properly and children need to be taught basic card playing etiquette – don't pick up your cards until all the dealing has been completed and make sure you don't show your cards to other players. The shuffler always gets another player to *cut the cards* before a deal is made – this means picking off a section of the face-down shuffled pack and placing this pile of face-down cards towards the dealer who then picks up the remaining section of cards and puts them on top of the *cut* section. This is done so the shuffler can never see what card is on the bottom of the pack.

Players should always play "in turn" with the turn going around the table clockwise. If a player *revokes* by playing out of turn, the card they put down must be left face up on the table. This card must then be played after other players have played their turn. If the card is the wrong suit then the player *revoking* must play a correct card. The incorrect card must be left face up on the table and then played as soon as the right suit has been led.

The first step must always be to explain the make-up of the standard pack of playing cards There are the 4 suits – Clubs, Diamonds, Hearts and Spades. It's good to always refer to the *suits* in this order (alphabetically as it happens but also the order of seniority when you come to playing **Bridge**). There are the *colour cards* – Jack, Queen and King – and the Aces which are usually the most powerful cards in the pack. Finally there are the numbered cards from 2 to 10. This makes 52 cards in all plus 2 jokers – the jokers often having functions as *wild* cards taking any value. Aces are usually *high* so the 2 is the weakest card.

Some General card-playing skills!

In a very real sense the playing of cards is a micro-version of life.. Each player faces an important decision each time their turn to play comes around. And this decision is open to scrutiny from the other players and potential disaster if it proves to be a silly mistake! How exactly does an inexperienced person make this decision? How difficult might it be for beginners to learn to take this responsibility on their own? This is the value of playing cards which require young people to figure out the best strategy in the face of many uncertainties and in a social environment where silly mistakes can be embarrassing.

In some games, very little choice is required but in others there will be many factors to think about. When we are talking about *trick-taking* games like **Whist** and, ultimately, **Bridge** then the importance of *trumps* and *voids* becomes paramount.

Counting the cards!

In all the *trick-taking* games (the **whist** family and, finally, **Bridge**) the management of the *trump* suit is a key skill players must learn. (Cards of the t*rump* suit will always win the trick when players are able to play them if they have a *void* in the suit which has been played/led.) So from the very first games of, for example, **German Whist** or **Hearts** the young players should be encouraged to *count the trumps.* There are, of course, 13 *trumps* in the pack so each time a *trump* is played players will try to "keep track" by remembering how many have been played. This is just one single number to keep in your mind as the game progresses. When you combine that number with the number of *trump* cards you hold in your own hand you will have a good assessment of what *trump* cards the other players hold. These numbers will give you important signals on what strategy might be best in the playing of your remaining cards.

As players become more experienced and capable, they can begin to keep in their minds more and more information about what cards have been played. It is very helpful to strategy planning if you know, for example, that the Ace of a suit has been played when you are holding the King. Humans have good brains and they soon figure out for themselves the value of remembering cards. They also learn the value of *playing out trumps* if they hold the top cards of the *trump* suit in their own hands. By leading out the top cards in the *trump* suit you will force all the other players to get rid of *trump* cards which could pose potential problems as the game progresses. The decision on whether or not to *play out trumps* is one of the most significant in all games where *tricks* are taken.

Playing out Trumps

There are few things more annoying (in **Whist** type games) than to play the top card in a *non-trump* suit only to find it beaten by the 2 of *trumps*! One way of trying to avoid this is to "play out trumps". You can do this by leading a *trump* card (preferably a high one) when you have the lead. This means all the other players must play a *trump* card too. Make this lead a couple of times and you will likely *play out* all the trumps and, in this way, avoid the danger of other powerful cards you hold being *trumped.* You can *play out trumps* most effectively if you have taken the trouble to count the number of *trumps* played.

Managing a *Void*

Because the use of *trumps* is so important in many games of cards, players need to understand how powerful it can be to have a *void* (no cards) in a particular suit. In some games you may be passing cards (face down) to other players (in **Hearts** for example) so you can manage to make a *void* this way. In other games you may achieve a *void* by making careful discards. In **German Whist** you may make a *void* by careful choice of which cards to lead after you have won a *trick*....and so on.

Understanding *Distribution*

Although it may seem pretty obvious, card players need to realise that if the *distribution* of suits in their hand is peculiar (un-balanced) then it stands to reason that the same will be true in the hands of other players. This applies to all W**hist** type games. You might imagine, for example, that in a perfect world the distribution of suits in a 13-card hand might be 3,3,3,4 – which gives each suit more or less the same chance of being in the hand. So if your hand has a very skewed distribution – say 7, 4, 2, 0 – then it follows that the other players' hands must also be skewed. It's surprising how often players forget this as they luxuriate in the excitement of what seems like a wonderful hand only to discover that other players have equally unusual hands!

It is an interesting exercise to calculate the relative chances of dealing 13-card hands with different distributions. This is a straightforward mathematical exercise. The most common distribution is in fact 4,4,3,2 and this happens about once in every 5 hands dealt. Three hands out of ten will hold no more than a 4-card suit. The chances of holding one 5-card suit are about 2 in every 5 hands (0.43), the chances of holding one 6-card suit are about one in 7 hands (0.16), the chances of holding a 7-card suit are about one in 30 hands and the chances of holding an 8-card suit are one hand in 250. You would have to deal a hand of 13 cards every minute for 2 million years to have a chance of getting a hand with all 13 of a single suit!

6. LAST CARD – A GOOD PLACE TO BEGIN

This simple game is a good place to begin your kid's adventure in card-playing. Apart from having fun, the aim is to get the players used to the names and shapes of the 4 different suits, the numbers and the colour cards. There are a number of variants to this game which can make it more interesting but we start here with the basic game.

The pack is shuffled and 5 cards dealt out to each player. Between 3 and 8 people can play this game. All players make their cards into a fan and make sure none of the other players can see them. The remaining cards are placed face down in a pile in the middle of the table. The top card in the face-down pack is turned over beside the pack so everyone can see it. The player to the left of the dealer begins the game by taking a card from his/her hand – this card must be either the same suit as the upturned card on the table or the same number. He/she puts this card down face-up on the card which is already face-up beside the pack. If the player has no cards that fit these requirements then he/she picks up the top card in the face-down pack. If this card matches the suit or number it can be put down – if not it is added to the player's hand.

The next player to the left now takes his/her turn. The aim is to get rid of all the cards in your hand – the winner being the first one to do so. BUT no-one can win the game unless they announce to the group that they have reached the *Last Card* when they hold only one card left. They must shout this out as soon as they reach this point. If they fail to say *Last Card* before the next player takes his/her turn then they cannot finish and must pick up a card (as penalty) in their next turn. They cannot put down the single card they hold but they can put down the pick-up card if it is the right suit or number. Once again, if they are left with one card they MUST say *last card* to win.

There is an element of skill in the game because players may be able to guess or figure out what suits the player to their left is holding. The idea is to make it as difficult as possible for the next player to discard cards he/she is holding. If the face-down pack is exhausted before anyone wins then the discard pack is picked up, shuffled and put back down so the game can continue.

Once the young players have got used to the rules you can easily make the game more fun. For example, you can include the 2 jokers in the pack and make them and all the 2's in the pack *wild cards*. When a player holds a *wild* card he/she can nominate what suits the wild card represents (potentially making it easy for his/her next turn and more difficult for the next player). When a *wild* card is played the player may also require the direction of play to be reversed so the next player becomes the player on his/her right instead of the left. A player may not use a *wild* card as his/her last card.

When this more complex version has been mastered there is another way to make the game more challenging by scoring each hand according to the card values held by each player when the round finishes. The player who has won the round by saying *Last Card* and then being able to put this card down on his/her next turn will score zero. All other players then add up the numerical values of the cards remaining in their hands – colour cards count 10 and Aces 15. The scorer then writes down each player's score and totals up by adding together the player's previous scores. At the outset of the game, the group decide what total (for example 60 points) will bring the game to an end. At this end point, the player with the lowest total score is the winner. In this way there may be several rounds of play before a winner appears.

This final version of the game provides another level of simple challenge – keeping one's score and making sure to discard high-value cards first.

7. BEGGAR MY NEIGHBOUR

This is normally a game for two players unless more than one pack of cards is being used. Remove the jokers.

It is a great game to pass the time with occasional excitements and finally a winner - but no brain power or thought of any kind is required. The aim of the game is to force your "neighbour" (the other player(s)) to give you all his/her cards – so the winner holds the entire pack and none of the other players have any. The way this is done is through the ACTION cards (colour cards or Aces) which are buried in each player's pack.

To start the game, the pack(s) are shuffled and then split more or less equally between the players, keeping the cards face down. Each player now has a similar-sized pack of face-down cards in front of him/her. The face-down packs do not have to be exactly the same size because their value lies in the number of ACTION cards rather than the plain number cards. You won't know how many action cards you have until the cards are actually played.

Play is started by the player to the left of the shuffler. He/she takes the top card from his/her pack, turns it over and puts it down in the centre of the table/group so all players can see it. This card may be a simple numbered card of any suit or it may be an ACTION card (Jack, Queen, King or Ace).

When a simple numbered card has been played the next player to the left simply puts his/her next card down on top of the first card and the turn moves on to the next player. The upturned pack builds up in this way until an ACTION card is played.

Whenever an ACTION card is played it immediately requires the next player to play a single card to cover a Jack, 2 cards to cover a Queen, 3 cards to cover a King and 4 for an Ace. When the appropriate number of single-number cards have been placed on top of the ACTION card then the whole upturned pack is picked up by the player who put down the ACTION card. All the cards in the upturned pack are now added to the base of the ACTION card player's pack. This is the way players "beggar their neighbour(s)" for cards! The successful ACTION card player now continues the game by playing the next card from the top of his/her pack.

If, however, another ACTION card is played as one of the cards required then the turn immediately moves on to the next player, who must add the number of cards required by the new ACTION card to the upturned pack. The player who played the active ACTION card will pick up the pack unless a further ACTION card appears - and so on.

Young players quickly realise that the ACTION cards you want to have are the Jacks because only one non-ACTION card is required before you can pick up the whole pack. Where the ACTION card is an Ace the chances of picking up the pack are much lower because another ACTION card may well appear before 4 cards have been played.

NOTE - This game can sometimes go on for a very long time to the point of tedium – or it can prove very exciting!

8. PELMANISM OR MEMORY

This simple game is entirely about memory! In its simplest form, the pack will be sorted, for example, into the 36 numbered cards by taking out the Aces and colour cards – you can leave in the 2 jokers, if you like, to make 38 cards.

To play the game, shuffle the 38 cards and lay them face down on the card table/floor. You could put them in 2 rows of 10 and 2 rows of 9 or you could simply mix them around in a random pattern (the straight lines will be easier to start with).

The first player simply chooses 2 cards from the scattered pattern and carefully turns each one over without disturbing the others. The 2 upturned cards are left for several seconds so every player can see them. The aim is to try and remember exactly where each card is when they have been replaced face-down. The objective is to turn over 2 cards which are the same number and colour – e.g. 2 red nines........ When a matching pair have been turned over the 2 cards are picked up and taken by the successful player who piles them up carefully as his/her pairs and then has another turn.

Each player takes turns to turn over 2 cards, leaving them upturned briefly before returning them to their positions face-down. Those with the best memories will find more matched pairs than the rest. When all the cards have been picked up, the one who has found the greatest number of matched pairs is the winner.

The game becomes more difficult when you use more cards and decide to play with a more jumbled-up layout.

It is extremely difficult to remember ALL the cards that have been turned over so it's often best simply to try and remember 4 or 5. You can make this easier if you remember cards that are in special positions (on a corner, for example). Perhaps you can make the challenge easier if you focus on remembering just the cards you have turned over yourself. And you might use your own plan – perhaps picking up cards in a line so you can remember the order. Or you could base your choices on, say, using a phone number well known to yourself.

9. KNOCKOUT WHIST

Whisht is the Northumbrian word which means "Hush" or "Be quiet!" This game can be played by up to 6 players.

INTRODUCTION TO BASIC WHIST

"TAKING TRICKS" - The aim of the **Whist** game is to *take tricks* by putting down the highest card as each player in turn plays a card which must always follow the suit of the first card played (*the lead card*). Ace is high, then King, Queen, Jack and 10,9......2.etc.

Jokers are removed before the shuffle and do not come into the game. Shuffle, cut and deal 8 cards to each player. They hold them in a fan so others cannot see them. The rest of the pack is placed face down and not used. Each player now studies his/her "hand". Players will find the game easier if they organise their hand into *suits*, red and black *suits* separating each other.

The player to the left of the dealer starts the round by trying to *take a trick*. He/she must choose which card to play on the basis of the best strategy he/she can come up with after looking at the strength of the cards he/she holds. The next player, to the left, now plays a card which must *follow suit* (be of the same suit as the *lead*) if that's possible.. If a player cannot *follow suit* then he must *discard* any card in his hand (probably the lowest) or, if *trumps* are in play, he/she can play a *trump* to win the trick.

The player who has put down the highest card (Ace being the highest card) *wins the trick* and picks up all the cards played in that round. These cards are his/her *trick* and they are put, face down, beside him/her on the table. This becomes the start of that player's pile of *tricks*. It's best for players to keep their *tricks* beside them neatly so they can keep track of the number of tricks they have taken.

The player who has *won the trick* then *has the lead.* He/she has the advantages of playing the first card in the next *trick* (having what we call *the lead*). And so it goes on until all the cards in each hand have been played.

The "taking tricks" sessions need to be repeated a few times so every player has a clear idea of how it works.

The player with the most tricks at the end of the 8-card round wins the round. If 2 players finish with the same number of tricks then a *draw* must take place to decide the winner.

The *draw* is done by shuffling the pack and spreading the cards out, face down, so each player can choose one. The player choosing the highest card wins the draw. If 2 cards are drawn with the same numerical value then the card with the highest scoring suit wins (the order is first spades, hearts, diamonds and finally clubs). Kids often find the *draw* one of the most exciting parts of this game!

TRUMPS

Once the players have a good feel for playing the cards without *trumps* then the idea of *trumps* can be introduced.

Before the cards are dealt, the dealer chooses the trump suit by drawing a card at random from the pack. The suit of this card is nominated as the trump suit – all cards in that suit will be *trump cards* when the hands have been dealt.

Trumps are important because if a player does **not have any cards** of the suit (a *void*) which has been led he/she is able to play a *trump* of any size to win the trick. If two players (or more) play *trumps* then the one playing the highest *trump* wins. *Several hands should be played with trumps so that the players get the idea.*

PREPARING FOR THE KNOCKOUT GAME

Players begin the game by shuffling the pack and *drawing for deal*. The player drawing the highest card is the dealer. The aim of the game is to win as many tricks as possible. The player that "wins" the first 8-card round with the most tricks is the player who will choose the suit to be trumps in the next round. He/she makes this choice once the hands have been dealt and the players have looked at their hands. This "winning" player will also have the advantage of playing the first card when the next round begins (having the *lead*).

Eight cards are dealt in the first round, 7 in the second, 6 in the third ….and so on until the players have just one card each. The player who wins the last round wins the game!

THE KNOCKOUT GAME

The first hand in the game is played with No Trumps and 8 cards dealt to each player – as before. At the conclusion of the first round, the winner who has won the most tricks gets the right to choose the suit which will be "trumps" in the next round. He/she does this AFTER the next round has been dealt and players have picked up their cards.

Any player who does not get any tricks remains in the game after the first no-trump stage. ***In the following stages, players who win no tricks are "knocked out" and take no further part in this game (= "off to bed" in some households!).***

The second round of the knockout game is dealt with ONLY 7 CARDS. This time there are trumps chosen by the winner of the first no-trump round. The third round has only 6 cards dealt – and so on with one less card for each subsequent deal. Each round has the winner of the last round choosing trumps when the next round has been dealt. The process continues until only one player is left as the winner.

A STORY!

Here is a little story which may demonstrate just how effective a little card playing experience can be when dealing with super-bumptious chief executives. This happened 25 years ago and it features one of my daughters who was then 7 years old. My children were (and are) very familiar with the cut and thrust of competitive cards and they are calmly confident in their own ability to "shorten the odds" when trying to win. On this evening we had just entertained a visiting "chief executive" at a supper around the family table (5 of us at the time). After supper the children wanted to play cards - **Knockout Whist** - as they often did. The chief executive said he would play.

The loud chief executive was in a rather patronising frame of mind and clearly felt he should not be too forward in trying to win the game. As the rounds of deals progressed, our numbers declined (as they always do in knockout whist) until, rather dramatically, only my young daughter and the chief executive were left with one card each. The chief executive had won the last round and so it was his turn to choose *trumps*. As the two combatants faced each other there was a pregnant silence – what suit would the chief executive choose?

To our surprise he did not choose immediately but, looking my daughter straight in the eye, he asked "what colour is your card?". Now this was a tactic rather "below the belt" and not in the spirit of the game. Without hesitation my daughter said "it's black". "Right then" said the chief executive "I'm choosing hearts". He put down the 7 of hearts with a smug smile on his face only to be immediately dumbfounded when my daughter calmly put down the 10 of hearts to win the trick and the game. It had never occurred to this pompous fellow that a small child could so calmly outsmart his attempted plan. With a few years of experience in games, it had taken her only a moment to trick the poor fellow. Unlike my kids, the over-confident fellow could not cope with such a reverse and stomped off in a sulk.

10. GERMAN WHIST

This is a game best suited to 2, 3 or 4 players. A full pack of cards is used without the jokers. You will need to take out the 2 of clubs if 3 players are playing or the numbers will not work out when you deal the cards!

For children it's best to deal hands of, say, 7 cards each – you can do more or less depending on how well the kids can manage their cards.

When the cards have been dealt, the rest of the pack is placed face-down on the table and the top card turned over and placed beside the face-down pack. The suit of this upturned card will be the *trump* suit for the rest of the game.

The players are holding their cards so they cannot be seen by the others and they will normally sort the cards into suits – for ease of playing and planning.

The player to the left of the dealer opens play by leading (playing) any card of his/her choice. The other players must then follow suit and the player playing the highest value card *wins the trick.* If a player cannot follow suit then he/she may either discard any card or play a *trump* to win the trick. The winning player turns the cards in the *trick* face-down (so their suit and number must be remembered rather than being visible to players planning their next play). The *tricks* are set down beside the players who win them so everyone can see how many *tricks* have been taken – they know who is winning and who is losing!

After each *trick* has been taken, the winner of the *trick* picks up the card which is face-up beside the face-down pack in the centre of the table. The other player(s) take the top card from the face-down pack. So after each round has been played all the players still have the same number of cards as they started with. The person who wins the trick has the lead for the next round – and so the process continues until all the face-down cards have been picked up. The last few cards are simply played from the players' hands as before. The winner of the game is the player with the most tricks after all cards have been played.

STRATEGY

The player who has the most *trumps* has a very big advantage in this game. This is especially true in the final stages of the game when all the cards in the central pack have been taken. You can, with clever play, build up the *trumps* you hold in your hand by winning tricks when the exposed "pick-up card" is a *trump.* Equally, you can avoid winning when the "pick-up card" is of very low denomination.

This game is an ideal format for teaching the children to *count trumps*. You want to make this process become a secure card playing habit. There's just one number to remember – the number of *trumps* that have been played. When you know this number you can plan the final phase of the game much more effectively – deciding either to play out *trumps* (if you have the most) or use your *trumps* to win tricks by trumping in the suits where you have a *void.*

11. OH HELL!!

A simple but testing game for up to 7 players – a great way of learning to manage your cards with *trumps* and *voids*.

13 hands will be dealt to make a complete game (see below) – time taken about 1 hour.

1. In the first hand 7 cards are dealt to each player and *trumps* are nominated as being "clubs". (Trumps will change in each subsequent hand according to the following sequence – clubs, diamonds, hearts, spades and finally no-trumps. The cards will be played to *take tricks* as in the normal rules of **Whist** (players must follow suit and can only trump in they have a *void* in the suit played).
2. Players look at the cards in their hands and organise them – with the aim of trying to decide how many tricks they will make when the hand is played out. The scorer writes these down to keep a record.
3. Each player (starting at the left of the dealer and rotating clockwise after each deal) announces how many tricks he/she will try to make. The scorer writes down the number for each player. The last player to announce his/her trick number MUST choose a number which does not make a total equal to the number of cards to be played in that hand (so somebody must fail to achieve their target!) Some groups do not like using this rule – so you can make your own decision about this.
4. The player who made the first announcement has to lead for the first trick.
5. Tricks are played out in the normal way.
6. At the end of the round, players tell the scorer whether or not they have achieved their target – if "yes" then they receive 10 points plus 5 points for the number of each

tricks successfully declared. If they fail to get their target number of tricks (over or under) they receive no points.

7. In the next hand, the same procedures are followed but one less card is dealt. Again each player must announce the number of tricks he/she expects to make. Scoring is done as before.
8. Each subsequent hand has one less card dealt – each hand is scored as before. Finally when each player receives only 1 card he/she must NOT look at it but place it against his/her forehead facing the other players. Play then proceeds as before with each player having to make an educated guess as to what he/she is showing to the others!
9. After the one-card round, the number of cards in each deal is increased by 1 for each subsequent deal – all being scored in the same way. When 7 cards are again dealt to each player this is the final round, after which scores are totalled and the winner announced.

12. HEARTS

This is a game to be played by between 3 to 5 players. A full pack is used without the jokers. The 2 of clubs should be taken out for the 3-player game and the 2 of diamonds as well if 5 players are involved. You must take these cards out so that the deal works out with these numbers of players. **Hearts** is a difficult game to master so some care must be taken to ensure players have already had decent experience with other **Whist**-type games before playing.

After the shuffle all the cards are dealt out to the players. The rules of *trick taking* as in **Whist** will apply and the aim of the game is to take as many tricks as possible WITHOUT including any hearts in the cards taken in those tricks. This may sound simple but, in practice, it can be extremely challenging.

Normally 5 successive hands will be dealt to make up the whole game with the trump suit for each successive deal being set at Clubs, Diamonds, Hearts, Spades and finally No Trumps. Note that this order of trumps mirrors the pecking order of suits used in the more sophisticated game of **Bridge** which the kids may eventually aspire to.

You will need a pencil and paper to keep the score in this game! Scores are worked out for each player after every hand has been played. Ten plus points are scored for each trick taken, 20 plus points are given if the Jack of Diamonds is in those tricks, 20 negative points are taken off if the Queen of Spades is in those tricks and negative points are taken off for every heart card in the tricks. The negative hearts points are scored using the value of the card as the scoring value with colour cards counting 10 and the Ace counting 15. (Players may vary the basis of scoring if they want to change the dynamic – for example by making tricks count more to encourage positive play.)

The "pass-on"

Crucially before the play begins after the deal (whilst the players are all holding their cards carefully so they cannot be seen by others), each player must pass either 3 cards (in the case of the 3-player game) or 2 cards (in the 4 or 5-player games) face-down to the player on their left. This must be done by all the players without looking at the cards they have been passed by their neighbour. Passing on the Queen of Spades is NOT permitted. The logic and dynamic of each game is very different depending on which suit is *trumps* – voids are extremely useful! A void allows you to dump nasty high-tariff cards on the tricks taken by your opponents. Leaving yourself with too many trumps may become a serious embarrassment in the later stages of the game – the point where everybody is trying to get rid of their hearts!

Once the cards have been passed on, play begins with the lead being to the left of the dealer. Cards are played in sequence, following suit where possible as in **Whist**, with the highest card winning the trick. *Trumps* are used in the same way as in all **Whist-**type games. Those who are able to take *clean* tricks (without hearts or the queen of spades) are most likely to win.

Heart leads are controlled

It is an essential rule that no heart can be led until a heart card has been discarded. This rule is important. Once hearts have been played there is likely to be a "heart war" where those with very low hearts choose to lead them to force the players holding higher cards to take the *trick*. Once you have experience in this game you will find that the most valuable cards in the game are the 2, 3 and 4 of hearts. If you hold any of these low heart cards you will have insurance against the dangers of the "heart wars".

When all the cards have been played, the players' scores are added up and marked down on the score sheet. After 5 hands – each with a different suit as *trumps* – the game ends and the player with the highest score is the winner.

13. WHIST – A GAME FOR 4 PLAYERS

Players sit in two pairs with partners facing each other. Each pair is a "team" and will try to help each other win *tricks* during the game. Players must know how to *take tricks* (see **Knockout Whist**) before they begin to play the full game of **Whist**. They must know about t*rumps,* too.

The dealer is chosen by drawing cards. All cards are dealt out (without the jokers) so each player holds 13 cards, facing towards him, in his/her hand. Players should be taught to organise their hands, arranging the cards into their suits from highest to lowest and separating the reds from the blacks. This makes the game easier to play.

The player to the left of the dealer makes the first *lead* - his/her partner needs to take careful note as a player will often lead a low card of a suit he/she wants the partner to lead back to him.

Throughout the first deal, Clubs are the suit nominated as *trumps* for all 13 tricks. Either player in a pair can *win the trick* for his/her side. When all 13 *tricks* have been taken the number of tricks for each side are counted – these are noted down as the *score* for each side.

Five separate *hands* or *deals* will take place to make a game. In the first deal Clubs are trumps, in the second Diamonds, the third Hearts, the fourth Spades and the final hand No Trumps. (The order is alphabetical!) After all 5 hands have been played, the pair with the highest number of tricks are the winners.

TACTICS

Learning to play in pairs is tricky. Players must try to figure out what, and why, his/her partner is up to. One member of the pair should normally play low while the other plays high – so as not to waste good cards. *Lead through strength to weakness* - so if you believe the player immediately to your left holds high cards in a particular suit, you will lead a low card of that suit to *squeeze* or *finesse*, hoping your partner will have a higher card.

Learning to *count the trumps* is the first essential to good play. In each hand there are 13 trumps. If a player *leads* a trump then it is likely that 4 trumps will be played in that round. So after 2 rounds of trumps 8 trumps are likely to have been played leaving 5 in players' hands. Three rounds of trumps might just work with 12 played but this is unlikely. If you know how many trumps there are in your own hand you can make a guess on where the others are. The person holding the dominant trumps towards the end of the game has a very strong position.

14. CANASTA

Canasta is not an easy game for younger kids – first, because you have to hold a lot of cards in your hand; second, because some of its nasty twists and turns can lead to tears. Two packs of cards are needed, including the 4 jokers. To win the game, players must collect cards of the same number – 7 cards make a canasta with jokers and 2s being “wild” (but your wild cards can never outnumber the real cards to make a canasta). A big part of the game for good players involves making sure the other players cannot easily collect the cards they want. This is why the game can get rather tense and I do not recommend it for youngsters for this reason.

The rules of **Canasta** are complicated and there are several different variants. Maybe teenagers would enjoy it so, if they want to play, you can look up the rules and get started. Here again, scoring can be quite challenging – there are a lot of numbers to add up.

15. BRIDGE

By the time you reach this chapter your young proteges should be completely at ease playing such games as **Oh Hell!** and **Hearts**. They will understand *distribution*, the importance of *trumps* and the value of *voids*. Probably they will be teenagers by now – and ready for the last great step in card-playing: **Bridge.**

The game of **Bridge** is possibly the most sophisticated and globally important card game of all! Thousands of books have been written about the game and there are thousands of clubs all over the world. In effect, **Bridge** is a huge global industry. All we can do in this book is give a brief outline of some of its main features – a way to get you started! **Bridge** is a big topic so take your time reading this through and don't be put off by what may seem like fearsome complexity.

It's a good idea to find some willing, experienced B**ridge** player to help your students get a grasp of this important but complicated game.

Let's get clear at the start that there are two forms of **Bridge**. In both forms, the cards are dealt and played in the same way but the scoring and formats are very different. The big club and international game is called **Duplicate** - the social game we play around the kitchen table is called **Rubber** (or **Contract**) **Bridge**.

Two Different Games of Bridge – Duplicate versus Rubber

The game of **Bridge** evolved from a long history of **Whist-**type games which certainly began more than 300 years ago. At the end of the 19th century the format of **Whist** was developed and **Duplicate Whist** was already being played (where teams of 2 players meet other teams of 2 players and each team plays the same hands as all the other teams to see who can win best).

We are only going to deal in detail with **Rubber Bridge** here as this is a true *game* whilst **Duplicate Bridge** (where all the pairs play the same hands) is essentially a *test* to find out who has the best systems of bidding and playing regardless of the luck of the deal. In any case, **Duplicate Bridge** requires several teams of players and quite a complex system of "boards" (this is how the various deals are saved) and tables which enable the same hands to be played by all the teams. You cannot play **Duplicate Bridge** around the kitchen table! In what are highly competitive games, the players are not permitted to talk to each other and, in some cases, are not even allowed to see each other. It is altogether a serious business and not really a *game* in any normal sense of that word.

Just four players are needed to play **Rubber Bridge**. The players play in 2 pairs – your partner is the player sitting opposite you. The game is great fun – often played for small stakes of money. Good players with experience can "think on their feet" (*what's my partner trying to tell me*!) and enjoy the social and psychological cut and thrust of the play.

Bridge is a trick-taking game, just like the **Whist** games we have already seen. In some respects it resembles the dynamic of **Oh Hell** because players must make *bids* before they play the hands. The *bid* is something like an educated guess on how many tricks the pair "winning" the contract hope to get with their chosen suit as trumps. "Winning" the contract refers to the end point of the bidding process where neither side feels able to bid any higher. For example, the *contract* might be a bid of 4 hearts – say – this means the pair "winning" the bid must take 10 tricks (4 + 6) with hearts as trumps.

Right from the start it's important for players to understand and learn how the scoring is done. Each player should have their own score sheet. The sheet is divided by a vertical line down the middle so that the scores on the left hand side are denoted *we* and those of the opposition (on the right hand side) are denoted *they*. There is a double line ruled horizontally across the middle of the score sheet – points scored "below the line" count towards "game" whilst those above are bonus or penalty points. The complete game or *rubber* ends when one pair has won two games (best of three) at which stage all the points are added up to see which side has won (and by how much). You can only gain points below the line by winning a contract. When one side has scored 100 points plus *below the line* they have won one game and a line is drawn right across the score sheet so any *below the line* points achieved by the other pair no longer count towards game. The side winning a game becomes *vulnerable* which means any penalty points they suffer are more than doubled (an effective deterrent to reckless bidding). Sides incur penalty points when they fail to achieve their contract number of tricks – we say they are *down in their contract.*

Bidding!

The process of *bidding* has developed and evolved over decades so there are many complex conventions which aim to provide information about the distribution and strength of the cards in the bidder's hand. There is a *Beginners Guide* to bidding conventions at the end of this chapter. New players might find it helpful to copy this and keep it near at hand when they begin to explore this game.

In the game of R**ubber Bridge** the emphasis is first on winning *games* (getting 100 points plus *below the line*) and second on getting your opponents *down* in a contract which they have played badly or which they should never have got into in the first place. N**ote** that bidding systems used for **Rubber Bridge** differ substantially from those used in **Duplicate Bridge.** This is because in the **Duplicate** game the emphasis is on getting into the best contract possible using the same hands which are played by all the other pairs. In **Rubber Bridge** it is getting a game score which matters. Beginners should bear this in mind when they begin to research alternative systems. The complex bidding systems developed for **Duplicate Bridge** are both unnecessary and risky in **Rubber Bridge**. *Over-tricks* (getting more tricks than your contract requires) are of little importance in **Rubber Bridge** because it is the simple 100 points for *game* that matters. When sophisticated bidding systems go wrong the mistakes can be very costly!

The *contract* we talk about in **Bridge** is the "bet" or "agreement" which one set of pairs makes in the hope (and belief!) that they can play out the hand and win the exact (or at least greater) amount of tricks they had bid for. The contract is played out by the *declarer* (the person who made the first bid of the trump suit – or No Trumps – which wins the contract. The declarer's partner is the *dummy* and plays no part in the game (other than making the tea!).

Playing Rubber Bridge

In **Bridge** the cards are dealt and played in almost exactly the same way as in 4-handed **Whist**. Each player is dealt 13 cards and 2 pairs compete in trying to win the optimum number of tricks which their combined hands will allow. So far this is the same as **Whist** – but in **Bridge** the number of tricks which the sides must play for, and the suit which is to act as trumps, are chosen by the process of *bidding*.

The player who has dealt the cards makes the first bid – the *opening bid*. He/she must assess the strength of his/her hand and decide on this basis how many tricks may be made. If the hand seems strong enough to make more than half the tricks (i.e.7 or more) then a player may make an *opening bid* which is announced so all players can hear. If the hand has a suit with 5 or more cards (say spades) then the player is likely to *open* with a bid of "one spade". This is, in effect, a bet that this pair could make at least 7 tricks with spades as trumps. If the hand is not strong enough (we will discuss this later) then the player simply announces a *no bid* - and the next player is called upon to bid. The bidding can go all around the table but each bid must be higher than the one before (as in any auction).

As we have already said, the suits are ranked in strength alphabetically – weakest being Clubs, then Diamonds, Hearts, Spades and finally No Trumps. A bid of one club can be followed by a bid of one of any other suit. So a bid of 1 spade can only be followed by a higher bid – either 1 No Trump or 2 of any other suit (bidding 2 of a suit means trying to win 8 (2+6) tricks or more).

The process of bidding continues until there are 3 consecutive no *bids*. At this point the "contract" is decided – setting the number of tricks that must be taken with the chosen suit as trumps. The player who will play the hand to try and achieve the contract is the player who made the first bid in the suit which is to be trumps. This player is called the *declarer*. If the opponents believe the contract is too ambitious they can *double* the contract. A *doubled* contract has a doubled score if the declarer succeeds and a doubled penalty if he/she fails.

Once bidding is over then playing of the hand begins. Here again **Bridge** differs from **Whist** because only one player (the *declarer*) of the pair with the contract actually plays the hand. The partner (sitting opposite the declarer) is the d*ummy* and takes no part in playing the hand.

As we have said, the declarer is the person who first bid the suit which is being played as trumps. The player to the left of the declarer makes the first lead in the game. This opening lead is extremely important – often deciding the outcome of the play (we'll talk about this later). Once the first lead has been made, the *Dummy* lays his/her hand face-up on the table – usually with the trump suit laid on the right-hand side. The cards in d*ummy's* hand are face-up on the table and will be played by the d*eclarer*.

The *dummy* must not touch the cards or influence the play except at the specific request of the declarer.

The fact that all players can see the dummy hand is a big factor affecting choice of strategy as the cards are played. It's also useful to remember the detail of the bidding – this may give a clue as to what cards are being held in the hands of other players.

How to count your point score to guide your bidding according to "convention"

The colour cards are scored with points as an aid to bidding. Point scores: Ace=4, King=3, Queen=2, Jack=1. In addition you can count a Singleton=1 and a Void=2. Note that there are 40 points in a pack of cards – normally a pair would need at least 22 points to have any chance of making a viable contract.

Bidding has become a sophisticated way of giving information to your partner (and the opposition!) about your hand – there are whole books and University courses about bidding!! In **Rubber bridge** it is best to start with a simple system as follows. The important thing is not to confuse or mislead your partner or you will end up in the wrong contract.

Your Opening Bid

After arranging your hand carefully and taking a points count on the basis just described, you must make a decision on whether and what to *open the bidding*.

With 12 points or below - **do not bid** unless you have a 6 or 7+ card suit (see below)

13/14+ points and a 5-card suit - bid 1 of the Suit

13/14 points and no 5-card suit – bid 1 Club (often risky)

16/17 points plus stoppers but no 5-card suit - bid 1 No Trumps

18/19 points plus a 5-card suit - bid 2 of the suit

18/19/20 points (no 5-card suit) but stoppers in all suits - bid 2 No Trumps

21 + points - you must bid 2 Clubs (2 Diamonds is the negative response)

If you have a very long suit (6+) and little strength - bid 3 of the long suit. This is called a **"pre-emptive bid"** and no reply is expected from your partner.

Any "jump" bid (raising by 2 instead of 1) made is usually what is called a "forcing bid". This means your partner MUST reply unless the bid is already a *game call.*

Your Reply –

up to 6 points – no bid

7 – 9 points - raise with your best suit (normally the longest) but use clubs as a *take out* (i.e. please stop now....) or 2 diamonds to *take out* after a 2-Club opening from partner.

10 + points - think about forcing by jumping a bid (you do this by going up 2 steps in the bidding rather than one and it means you want to go for game)

Once the first round of bidding has taken place you should proceed very cautiously if the opposition has been bidding. If in fact they are the ones looking to make a contract then you do not have many options except to *pass*. Eventually you may consider a "double" (especially if they are vulnerable having won one game). Note that the penalty scores for undertricks can become very large when you are *vulnerable.* This is a strong argument for raising the minimum point count for your bidding. (In this sense *vulnerable* means exactly what it says – you had better be careful.)

If you have opened the bidding and your partner responds then the challenge is to see if you can find the best "fit" (which suit to choose as trumps – or No Trumps). You may want to show your partner that you have another strong suit – or you may simply keep the bidding going by re-bidding your original suit. **Note** that when your partner's initial response is simply to re-bid your original suit you should take this as a very weak bid – unlikely to lead to game.

Playing the cards

This requires practice. You must always count trumps. It's easy to count if you start with a clear foundation so....... remember the distribution in your own hand – i.e.4,3,3,3 If you remember this then you can look at the cards left in your hand and quickly see how many of each suit have been played. Remember that cards are very unlikely to go 3 rounds without being trumped!

Playing a contract means looking for suits you can establish - i.e. long suits. You must take gambles with what is called finessing. When high cards are on your left they are often likely to win but if they are on your right you may be able to *play through* from *dummy*. This way you opponents high cards will be beaten by the cards in your own hand. You may get information about where the high cards are by recalling how the opponents did their bidding.

Deciding when to "play out" trumps is critical – it's almost always a good idea to do this sooner rather than later UNLESS you feel you can use trump cards in the weaker hand to "cross trump". You can only do this if you have a shortage of cards in one suit (a doubleton or singleton). If you can engineer a *void* in this suit then "cross trumping" will make the best use of the trumps you hold.

Always remember that you often need to keep leads so you can get back onto the table – there is nothing worse than forgetting this and finding you are left with several winning cards in *dummy* that you cannot access. Remember – if you have an unusual distribution of cards then it is highly likely that the distribution in other players' hands may be similar in pattern to your own.

Playing good defence is critical to winning at **Rubber bridge**. This always requires careful thought as to what your partner is trying to tell you. The first lead in any hand is likely to be critical. If in doubt, lead trumps is not a bad motto! Remember to lead back to suits which your partner has led to you or suits which he/she has bid. It may be good to lead cards in the weakest suit held by the dummy – forcing the declarer to make difficult choices. It may be good to lead cards from a singleton or doubleton – this is one way to create a void where you can trump later. Remember to make life difficult for the opponents - for example by making him/her play high cards from *dummy* so potential leads are gone. And don't *finesse* your partner by playing through him/her to high cards on the table.

The cleverest way to win is to deceive the opposition as to the strength of your hand when they are vulnerable and trying to go for a game. This is why you must never be tempted to overbid a weak hand when vulnerable - always err on the side of caution.

Scoring in Rubber Bridge

Knowing how to score and constantly keeping an eye on the score is absolutely essential to playing good rubber bridge.

A *rubber* in bridge ends when one side has won the best of three *games*. At this point all the scores are added up and the side with the highest total score wins the rubber. The stakes players agree to play for must be decided before any cards are played. 50 years ago the common stake was one penny per hundred but in today's world 20p (or even 1£) per hundred might be more appropriate. With your kids you can use pretty counters as money! You might play with stakes where 1 counter is paid to the winners of the rubber for each hundred points they have grossed above the losers. You can begin your rubber bridge session by giving each player (say) 20 counters – so when one pair has lost all its counters the session is over!

My own preference for the kids is to start them with some real cash so that their success or failure is measured in REAL gains!

NOTE – If there are no stakes in the game then you may often find that players are tempted to make silly over-ambitious bids simply because they want the fun of playing hands (even losing hands).

How the scores are made

The bridge score card is divided into 4 sections. There is a vertical dividing line in the centre of the score sheet with a heading on the left side "WE" and a heading on the right side saying "THEY". You will write your own scores down on the left hand side and the opposition's on the right. This way you can always keep track of what is going on.

There is a horizontal double line across the centre of the score sheet. Scores from successful contracts which go towards *game* are written below this double line. They are "below the line" scores. You need 100 points below the line to get a game. Bonus scores and penalty points are scored above the line. These "extra" points do not count towards *game* but they often make a major difference to the final rubber score.

Contracts in Clubs and Diamonds score 20 points for each bid made. Hearts and Spades score 30 points each and No Trumps score 40 for the first and 30 for each subsequent trick (so 3 NT is a neat 100 game). All scores made in successful contracts are written below the line. If over-tricks are made then their value (at the same tariff) is scored above the line – so overtricks do not count towards *game* (but they will add to the final score at the end of the *rubber).*

At the end of the rubber (best of 3 games.... or when time runs out!) then a rubber bonus is added to the scores of the pair winning the rubber. 700 points are added for a 2 game rubber win, 500 points are added for a 2 versus 1 game rubber win and just 300 points are added (when time runs out) for the pair (if any) winning 1 game.

Penalty points

Players failing to make their contracts (being "got down") must concede penalty points to the successful defending pair. In rubber bridge these points are often the most important scores deciding who wins the rubber and by how much. This is because penalty points can become very large when a contract has been doubled or re-doubled against a pair that is vulnerable. You will often find a ready tariff setting out penalty points in bridge on a card inside any new pack of cards.

For a normal hand (not vulnerable or doubled) the penalty points are 50 for each trick below the contracted number – e.g. 100 penalty points if a side goes 2 down in their contract. If the contract has been doubled then these penalty points are also doubled. When a pair is vulnerable (having won a game) then any penalty points are significantly increased.

Always check the score before you decide what to bid. You can ask your partner what the score is but you cannot tell him or her to stop bidding! Asking for the score is usually a tacit signal to "shut up".

Being Vulnerable

Once you win a game (100 points below the line) then you are "vulnerable" and the penalty points if you "go down" are more than doubled. **This means you must add one or two points to each required point score for bidding. Getting high penalty points from your opponents is often the best way you win at rubber bridge.**

Sacrificial Bids

There are often occasions in rubber bridge where it can beneficial

(on a balance of probabilities) to make a sacrificial bid. This is a very different situation compared to the rigour of duplicate bridge. The objective of the sacrifice bid is to either prevent your opponents getting into a game contract that would score highly (perhaps by winning the rubber) OR to force them to risk attempting a more challenging higher contract (when you might benefit from doubling). You don't expect to make your contract with a sacrificial bid but you do expect your penalty point losses to be less than the
score which your opponents would have achieved by making their hope-for contract.

The pre-emptive bid is one common approach to making a successful sacrificial bid. You achieve this where your hand may not have sufficient point score to make a conventional opening bid but you do have at least a 6 card suit. Your opening (pre-emptive) bid will be at the 3 level – making it difficult for the opponents to find their best contract with conventional bidding. Your partner would need a very strong hand to make any response to a pre-emptive bid.

Tactics

Try to play safely and cautiously when trying to make your contract. Overtricks are worth very little in the rubber bridge scoring system (unlike duplicate).

You can afford to take risks when trying to make a tricky contract. It will be a big plus if you make it but only a relatively small (if not doubled) penalty if you don't.

When you are trying to get your opponents down in their contract you can afford to take risks – there is big advantage in getting them down and relatively little penalty if they do get overtricks.

16. POKER

Poker is the gambling game most commonly seen in old western films where the cheat gets shot amidst swirling clouds of cigar smoke and many green eye-shades. **Poker** is a big industry – like **Bridge** – and is played all over the world especially by sporting groups of men late into the night.

The primary reason for teaching your kids to play poker is so they do not get caught out as novices on some future social evening with hard drinking colleagues. You can lose a lot of money very quickly!

Poker comes in many different formats but the essential principles remain the same. You are betting the strength of your hand against the strength of all the others BUT (if you want to win big money) you must do this in a way which is unpredictable. The game is played with a normal pack (without jokers) and using counters of some sensible kind to represent money.

Generally a **Poker** hand consists of 5 cards. These may be dealt in different ways – sometimes the 5 may be chosen as best of 7, sometimes the 5 may include 3 open cards face-up for all to see. Not all **Poker** players will score the strength of hands in the same way – so it's a good idea to get this clear at the outset. A "straight flush" is the best hand – a run of cards all of the same suit. You then have 4 of a kind, a full house (3+2), flush (all same suit), straight (5 consecutive numbers), 3 of a kind, 2 pairs, a pair, and finally a single card (Ace high).

Generally those that wish to take part in a hand must "ante up" - that is put a minimum stake into the pot. The deal (of whatever kind) then begins. Sometimes play requires a fresh "ante" for each new card dealt -sometimes not – this depends on your game rules.

Once all the cards have been dealt then the betting begins. If you don't feel like betting then simply throw your hand in – face down. All you have lost is your "ante". If you want to keep your options open you can simply "check" (saying you want to stay in the hand for the moment until you see how many others bet and what they bet). Thirdly you can make a bet of whatever size you choose within the "pot limit". Other players wishing to stay in the game must then, in turn, follow your bet or, if they choose, raise it. If your bet is "raised" then you must add at least this "raised" amount to your next bid or you can, if you wish, raise again. When all players have put in amounts to meet the last raise and nobody has raised again, then all the hands are shown and the winning hand takes the whole pot.

The skills of **Poker** depend first on an accurate assessment of the strength of your own hand. This is a matter of probabilities and mathematics. Second, and perhaps more important, they depend on your skill in confusing other players as to whether you are bluffing or not when you make your bets. The more inconsistent and unpredictable you are then the more you are likely to win. A predictable player will never win big because everyone knows s/he will bet big when the hand is good so these other players will "fold" quickly without putting much into the pot.

Poker can certainly be fun and it's a good skill to learn but the sad truth is that the winners are generally those prepared to take the biggest risks. In the real money game, it is usually the richest who win the most. That is a fact your children should be taught to understand!

Your kids should learn early on (with real money) that playing this game can be disastrously expensive.

17. THE FINAL WORD

We have come to the end of our story. I am sure it will have been an interesting journey! Yes, I really do think that in so many ways our games of cards do mirror life. Whether we like it or not, we are all likely to face critical decisions where time is short and the balance of risks is unknown. Sometimes these decisions will be vital turning points in our lives (of course we only find this out later!).

Those people who understand the "ethos of the game" will be much better equipped to make "good" decisions at these critical moments. Life is not fair and it is certainly not predictable. The sooner our young people understand this, the better able they will be to act sensibly and effectively "when the chips are down".

This is the mission of this book. Card games are much more than "just fun". They provide an experimental arena for young people to explore some of the most fundamental realities of being alive in an uncertain world.

Good Luck!

Printed in Dunstable, United Kingdom

67568535R00037